Living Legacies With LaVeta

A COLORING ADVENTURE IN FINANCE

I0528508

This book belongs to:

_____

Presented by

Living Legacies With LaVeta

Printed in the USA

Cover & Interior Design by
Culture to Color®, LLC

For more information, visit
CultureToColor.com

To order your custom coloring book, contact
CS@CultureToColor.com
386-228-5147

WELCOME

Living Legacies with LaVeta: A Coloring Adventure in Finance
is a groundbreaking educational tool designed for parents, students,
teachers, and caregivers, aiming to impart crucial financial literacy
concepts in an enjoyable manner.

Similar to how a tree draws nourishment from its roots, our lives
flourish through our financial decisions. Within this coloring book,
we've incorporated natural landscapes to ground and relax you
as we embark on a captivating financial adventure.

This innovative coloring book merges fun and education, offering
a hands-on learning experience that engages participants of all ages
in actively shaping their financial understanding.

By combining the imaginative activity of coloring with financial
education, *Living Legacies with LaVeta* inspires confidence
and proactivity in users, ensuring they embark on a journey
toward a financially secure future.

In essence, this coloring adventure provides a valuable and enjoyable
approach to instilling financial literacy and making budgeting,
saving, and investing accessible and memorable.

SAVING SEASON

Efficiently managing monthly household expenses requires a deliberate approach to maximize savings.

- Start by **scrutinizing utility bills**, adjusting thermostat settings, and adopting energy-efficient practices to curtail electricity and heating costs.
- **Consider renegotiating contracts or bundling services** to secure better deals on internet, cable, or insurance, and use cashback apps or rewards programs while shopping.
- **Automate savings** by setting up direct deposits into a separate account. **Prioritize needs over wants** and resist impulse buying.
- **Tackle discretionary spending** by reassessing non-essential items. Opt for economical alternatives like homemade meals over dining out and explore free or cost-effective entertainment options.
- **Trim unnecessary subscription services** and redirect those funds towards savings.
- **Capitalize on budgeting tools or apps** to monitor expenditures, identifying additional areas for potential savings.
- **Create specific savings goals** to stay motivated.
- Lastly, **educate yourself** on personal finance to make informed decisions. Aim to allocate 5% to 10% of your income towards savings consistently to build a healthy financial cushion.

BUDGETING BLOOMS

Budgeting for your household expenses is crucial for several reasons:

1. Financial Discipline: Setting aside a specific amount for housing, home repairs/improvements, food, vacations, college planning, new car, wedding, investment property, hobbies, personal gifts, concert tickets, or outings helps you gain better control over your finances, preventing overspending in these areas. By consistently budgeting for these expenses, you develop better financial habits, potentially increasing savings and improving overall financial health.

2. Long-Term Planning: Budgeting allows you to plan for future goals, such as saving for a down payment on a house or setting money aside for a dream vacation. It enables optimization of resources by identifying areas where cost-saving measures can be implemented without compromising quality of life.

3. Stress Reduction: Knowing where your money is allocated eases stress. It provides peace of mind and stability, especially in times of economic uncertainty. It provides a clear overview of your expenses and ensuring stability in covering essential needs.

CULTIVATE YOUR CASH FLOW

Make more money when you can, while you can. Diversifying income sources can bolster household finances and pave the way for increased savings. Explore freelancing, seek part-time employment, or rent out property. Offer tutoring or engage in online surveys and investments. Drive for ride-sharing services, start a blog for advertising income, rent out tools through specialized platforms, and offer virtual assistance. These diverse income streams not only enhance financial stability but also empower households to work towards their financial objectives efficiently. Residual income or passive income can be generated through various avenues:

- **Investments:** Dividends from stocks, interest from bonds, or positive cash flow from rental properties.
- **Royalties:** Earnings from books, music, patents, or trademarks, etc.
- **Online Content:** Create digital products, courses, or monetize a blog or YouTube channel.
- **Affiliate Marketing:** Promote products/services and earn a commission on sales.
- **Create an App or Software:** Develop new programs, tools, and platforms to generate ongoing revenue.

Explore these options based on your skills, interests, and resources to establish a source of residual income.

INVESTMENT JUNGLE

Investing provides avenues for wealth growth. Each of these avenues have distinct characteristics and risk profiles.

- **Stocks** represent ownership in a company, offering potential returns through dividends and capital appreciation.
- **Bonds** are debt securities where investors lend money to entities in exchange for periodic interest payments and the return of principal at maturity, providing stable but lower-risk income.
- **Real estate** involves purchasing physical properties and generating income through rent or appreciation over time.
- **Mutual funds** pool money from multiple investors to invest in a diversified portfolio of stocks, bonds, or other securities, spreading risk.
- **Exchange-Traded Funds (ETFs)** are funds that trade on stock exchanges like individual stocks.
- **Certificates of Deposit (CDs)** are low-risk, time-bound deposits with fixed interest rates.
- **Precious metals**, such as gold or silver, serve as alternative investments, often acting as a hedge against inflation.

Understanding these various investment options allows individuals to tailor their portfolios based on financial goals, risk tolerance, and time horizons.

DEBT-FREE DOODLE

- **Start by creating a comprehensive inventory of existing debts,** including credit cards, loans, and outstanding balances.
- **Develop a realistic budget** that allocates a significant portion of income to debt repayment while ensuring essential expenses are covered.
- **Prioritize debts by interest rates or balances**, focusing on paying off high-interest debts first to minimize interest costs.
- **Consider negotiating** with creditors for lower interest rates. Embrace frugality by cutting non-essential expenses and redirecting those funds towards debt reduction.
- **Consistently make payments above the minimum required**, accelerating the debt payoff process.
- **Celebrate small victories** along the way, fostering motivation and commitment.

With persistence, a well-defined budget, and a commitment to financial discipline, individuals can steadily progress along the path to a debt-free destination, ultimately achieving financial freedom and peace of mind.

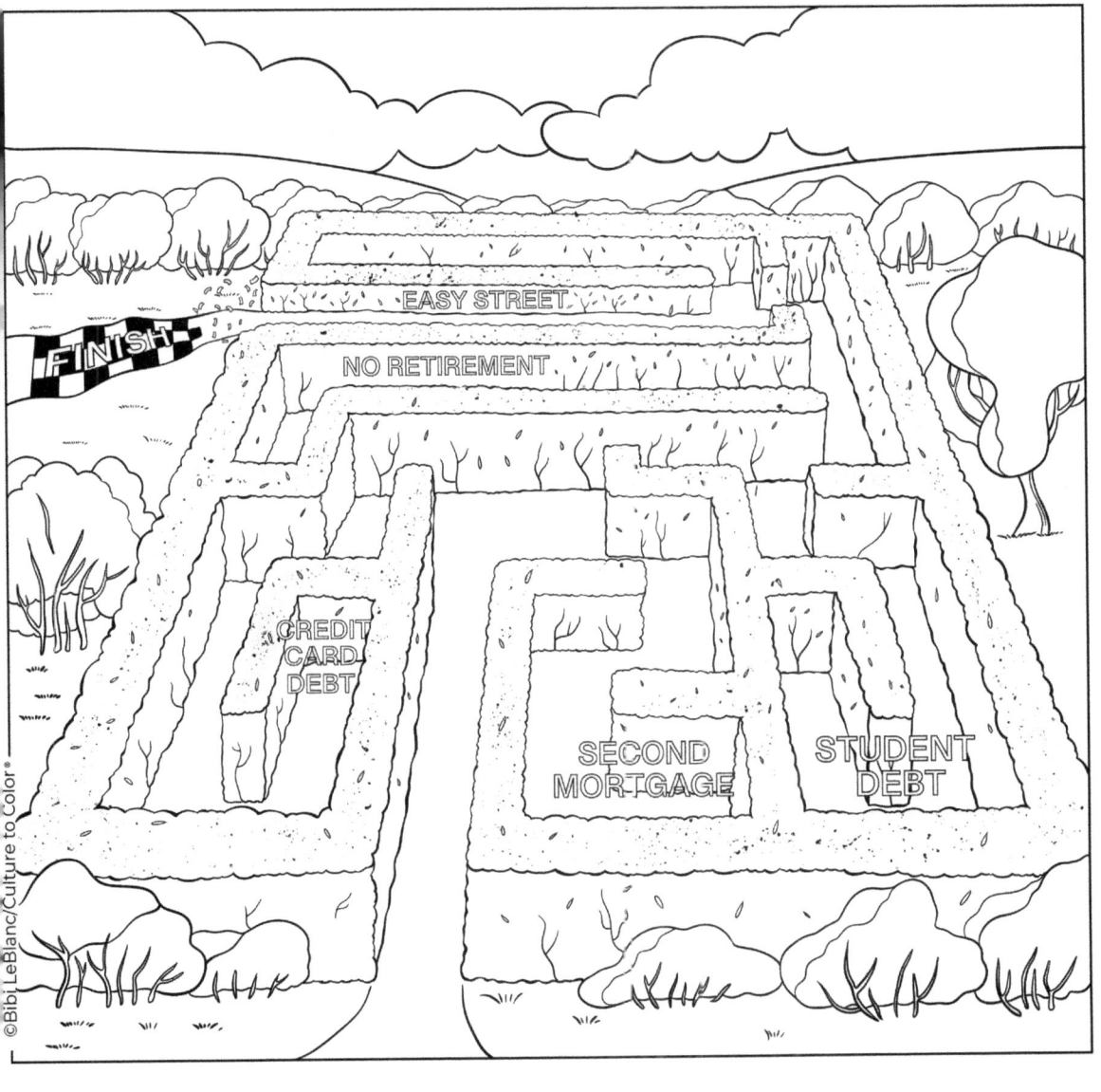

EMERGENCY FUND ESCAPE

An emergency fund acts as a financial safety net, providing a cushion against unexpected expenses or income disruptions. Imagine unexpected medical bills, car repairs, or sudden job loss—<u>the security provided by an emergency fund allows for financial resilience, ensuring stability in the face of life's uncertainties. An emergency fund is typically designed to sustain your life for three to six months</u>. LaVeta advises saving six months to one year worth of living expenses to ensure individuals or households have readily accessible funds to weather financial storms without resorting to high-interest debt or compromising daily needs.

- **Consider a scenario** where a natural disaster devastates your home, causing damages not covered by insurance. An emergency fund can cover these costs, mitigating the financial impact.
- **Build financial resilience** by establishing an emergency fund, providing a buffer against unexpected expenses.
- **Seek opportunities for supplementary income** through part-time gigs or freelancing.
- **Evaluate insurance plans** to ensure optimal coverage without unnecessary premiums.
- **Regularly revisit and adjust** the budget to align with evolving financial goals, ensuring a **continuous commitment to saving** within the household.

TAX-TIME ZEN

Navigating tax forms and documents can be approached with a sense of calmness by understanding the concepts of "tax now," "tax later," and "tax advantage."

- **"Tax now"** refers to immediate taxes on income, such as regular wages or interest earnings. While it requires timely payment, staying organized with clear records can alleviate stress during tax season.
- Conversely, **"tax later"** pertains to income or investments where taxes are deferred until a future date. Contributions to retirement accounts or certain investments fall into this category, providing a sense of relief as they allow for delayed tax obligations.
- **"Tax advantage"** involves strategically utilizing deductions, credits, and investment vehicles to minimize overall tax liability. Becoming familiar with these advantageous options, such as education credits or contributions to tax-advantaged accounts, empowers individuals to proactively manage their tax situation.

By categorizing income and understanding these tax concepts, individuals can approach tax season calmly, armed with the knowledge to optimize their financial strategy and navigate the intricacies of tax forms with confidence.

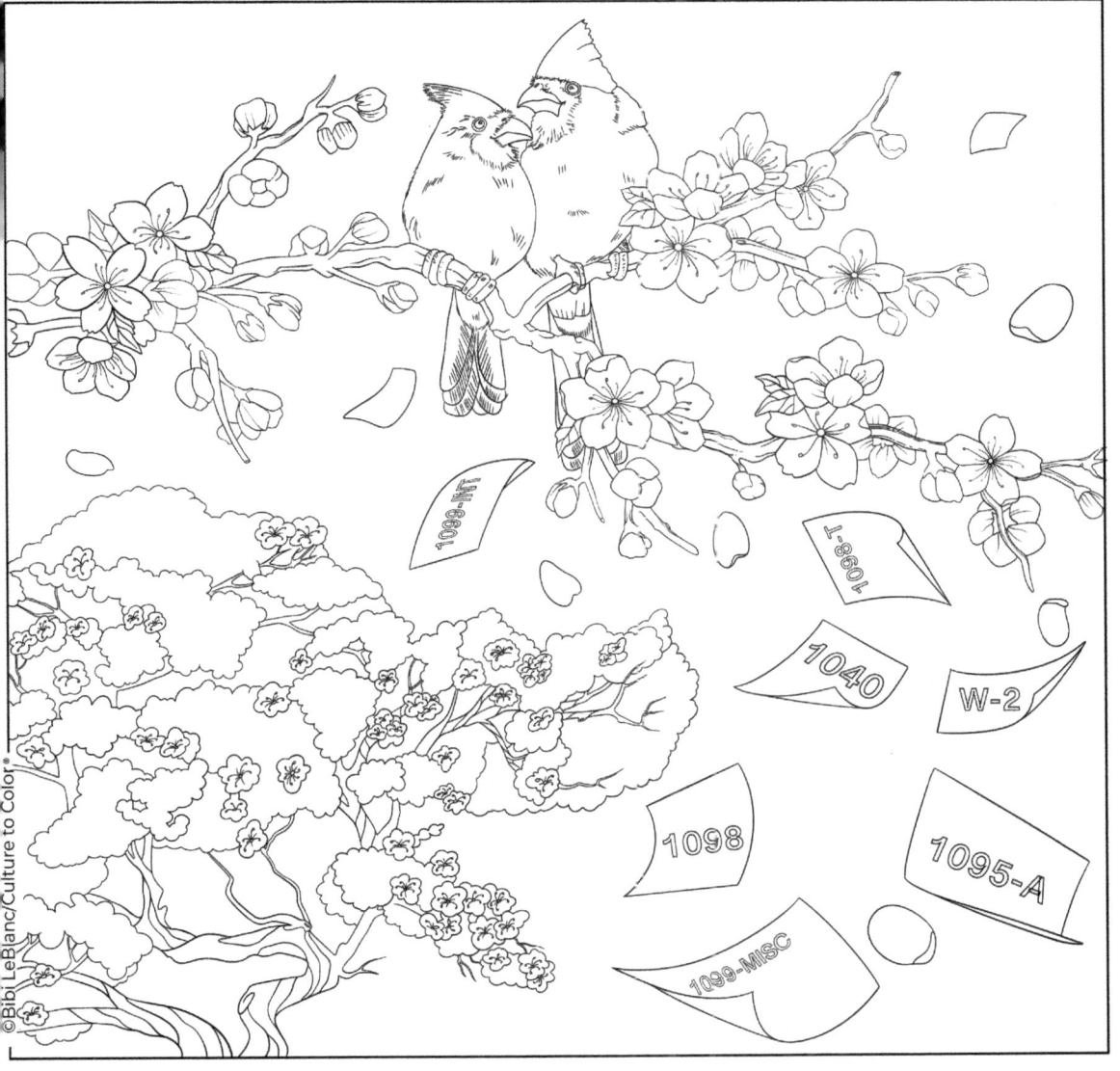

RULE OF 72

The "Rule of 72" is a handy financial concept for estimating <u>how long it takes for an investment to double in value</u>. To use it, simply <u>divide 72 by the annual rate of return, and you'll get an approximate doubling period</u>. For example, if you have an investment with a 6% annual return, applying the Rule of 72 suggests it will take around 12 years for your initial investment to double (72 ÷ 6 = 12).

This rule isn't limited to investments; it's versatile. You can also apply it to estimate how long it would take for high-interest debt to double. In this case, modify the formula slightly and use the annual interest rate on the debt. The modified formula is: Years to Double = 72 / Annual Interest Rate. Suppose you have a credit card with a 20% annual interest rate; the Rule of 72 indicates that it could take approximately 3.6 years for the debt to double (72 / 20 = 3.6). This highlights how high-rate debts can accumulate rapidly, emphasizing the importance of timely repayment to avoid significant financial burdens.

<u>Understanding the Rule of 72 empowers individuals to make informed financial decisions, whether in investments or managing debt. It underscores the power of compounding and the significance of interest rates in shaping financial outcomes</u>.

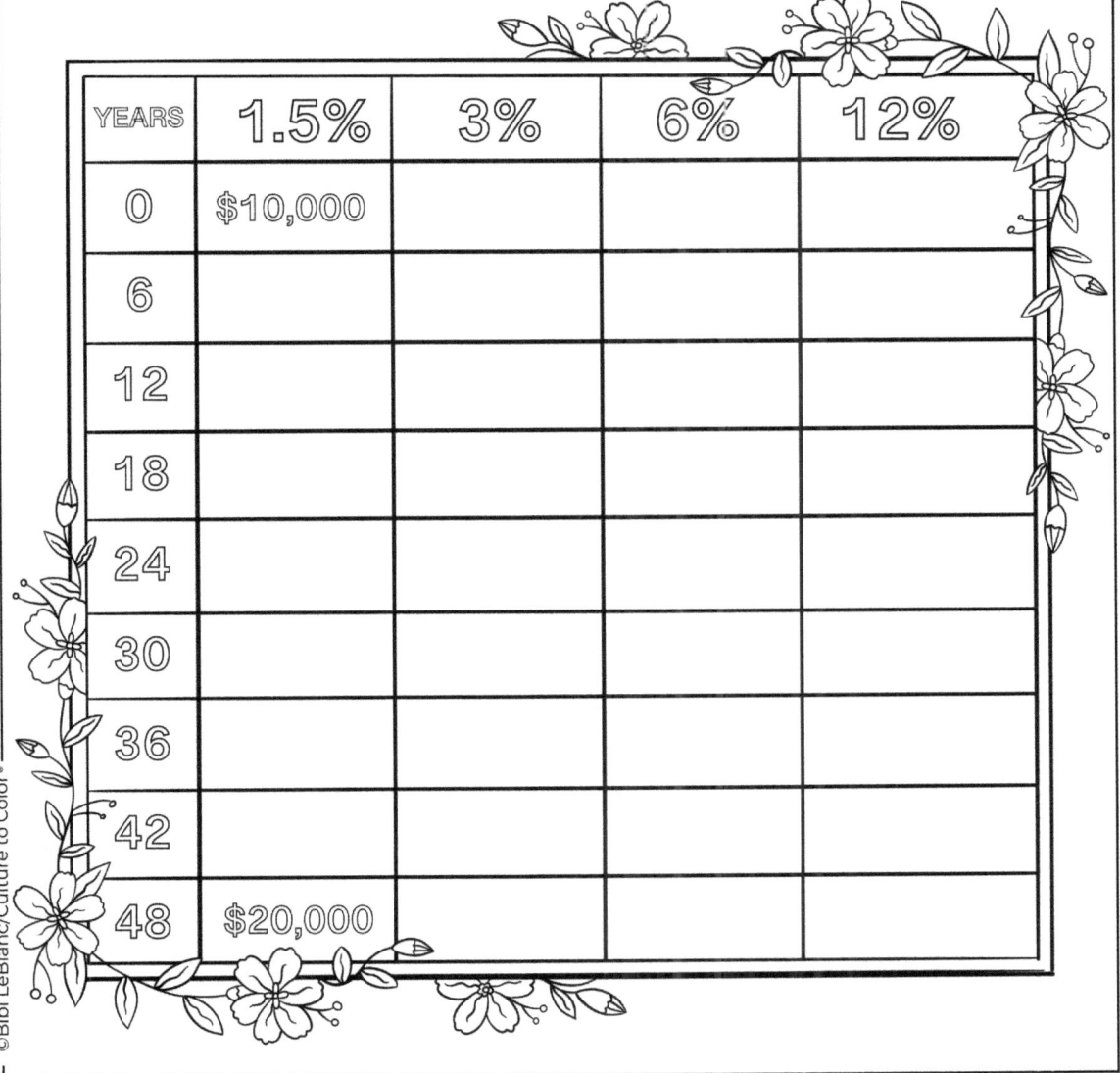

YEARS	1.5%	3%	6%	12%
0	$10,000			
6				
12				
18				
24				
30				
36				
42				
48	$20,000			

COLLEGE PLANNING

In the realm of "College Planning," engaging a College Coach is a valuable tool that extends beyond financial considerations. College coaches provide personalized guidance on the entire college application and selection process.

Their expertise includes:

Academic and Extracurricular Guidance:

- Course Selection: Assisting in choosing courses that align with academic goals and college requirements.
- Extracurricular Recommendations: Advising on activities that enhance the college application.

College Selection and Application Assistance:

- Researching Colleges: Helping students identify institutions that match their academic and personal preferences.

Application Support:

- Assisting with the application process, including essay writing and resume building.

Test Preparation and Strategies:

- SAT/ACT Guidance: Providing insights into test preparation strategies and when to take standardized tests.

Financial Aid Navigation:

- Scholarship and Grant Information: Identifying and applying for scholarships and grants to ease the financial burden.

By incorporating a College Coach into the planning toolkit, students gain personalized support, enhancing their chances of academic and personal success throughout the college journey.

RETIREMENT RELAXATION

By planning strategically, managing finances wisely, and investing sensibly, you can increase the likelihood of enjoying a comfortable retirement.

- **Start Early:** Begin saving and investing for retirement as soon as possible to benefit from compound interest.
- **Budget and Save:** Live within your means and save consistently.
- **Invest Wisely:** Diversify your investments to manage risk, and consider consulting a licensed financial professional for guidance.
- **Plan for Healthcare:** Factor in healthcare costs; consider insurance and savings for potential medical expenses.
- **Clear Debts:** Pay off high-interest debts to reduce financial burdens during retirement.
- **Estimate Expenses:** Estimate your retirement expenses to ensure you have enough saved to cover them comfortably.
- **Consider Downsizing:** Evaluate whether downsizing or relocating could reduce living expenses.
- **Stay Informed:** Stay updated on your retirement plan's performance and adjust it as needed.

FINANCIAL VISION BOARD

A "Financial Vision Board" is a powerful visual tool that combines the principles of a traditional vision board with financial aspirations. It involves creating a collage of images, words, and symbols, **representing one's financial goals and aspirations.**

The board serves as a tangible, personalized representation of the financial future an individual desires. Components may include **images of dream homes, travel destinations, investment goals, or symbols of financial freedom**.

By displaying this board prominently, individuals are reminded daily of their financial objectives, fostering motivation and commitment.

The process of creating a Financial Vision Board involves **introspection, goal-setting, and a creative expression** of one's desired financial reality.

Regularly updating and reflecting on the board can **enhance focus, align actions with goals, and serve as a dynamic roadmap** towards achieving financial success and fulfillment.

COLOR YOUR LEGACY

Leaving a colorful financial legacy involves meticulous planning and thoughtful utilization of tools to impact future generations positively. By incorporating these tools into financial planning, individuals ensure a vibrant and secure financial legacy, offering guidance and protection for future generations, and fostering a lasting impact beyond one's lifetime.

Life Insurance
Serves as a convenient and cost-effective way of leaving more wealth to the next generation.

Advanced Directives
Clearly state medical treatment preferences and end-of-life decisions.

Power of Attorney (POA)
Designates a trusted individual to make financial decisions on your behalf if incapacitated.

Will
Outlines how assets are distributed, ensuring one's financial wishes are honored.

Trust
Safeguards assets for beneficiaries and outlines conditions for distribution.

WHO WE ARE

LaVeta Hayes, a Daytona Beach native, received a Bachelor's in Accounting from Bethune-Cookman University and a Master's in Public Administration from Central Michigan University. With 37 years in the Federal Government, notably as Branch Chief of Financial Management Policy for the U.S. Forest Service, she excelled in financial management.

In 2019, she founded "Living Legacies with LaVeta, Inc." to honor her father, Edward "Creamy" Hayes, Jr., focusing on empowering individuals to manage and safeguard their finances, aiding countless clients in finance and insurance.

LaVeta specializes in Life & Health Insurance, Medicare, Estate Preservation, College and Long-Term Care Planning. Her goal is to foster trust-based relationships, offering lifelong tools for comprehensive financial success. Actively involved in organizations like Seminole County Chamber of Commerce, Crooms Academy Business Advisory Council, Bethune-Cookman University National Alumni Association, Delta Sigma Theta Sorority, Inc., and the Alumni Musicians Association, she's committed to community engagement.

Beyond her work, LaVeta cherishes travel, exploring diverse destinations worldwide, traveling to Africa, Asia, South America, and Europe, aspiring to cover all continents. She epitomizes professional excellence, championing financial education and legacy creation, leaving an enduring impact on individuals and communities.

CONTACT US

Living Legacies With LaVeta

703-283-2662

livinglegacieswithlaveta.com

L@livinglegacieswithlaveta.com

Follow us

(f) facebook.com/livinglegacieswithlaveta

(o) instagram.com/livinglegacieswithlaveta

(in) linkedin.com/in/livinglegacieswithlaveta

Benefits of Coloring

If you include coloring in your daily routine, you will find
it has many benefits for you, the coloring artist.
To name just a few, coloring can:

IMPROVE FOCUS

Coloring requires repetition and attention to detail. It opens up
your brain's frontal lobe, which controls organizing and
problem-solving, and allows you to focus on the activity
rather than your worries.

REDUCE STRESS AND ANXIETY

Coloring relaxes your brain's fear center (amygdala), putting you
in a state similar to meditation. Coloring helps remove
irritating thoughts and allows the creative mind to run free and relax.

IMPROVE SLEEP

Coloring as a bedtime ritual - instead of using electronics -
can lead to a better night's sleep. The light emitted by electronic devices
lowers the level of melatonin, your sleep hormone,
whereas coloring does not affect your melatonin level.

You can take coloring supplies anywhere. And you don't have
to be an artist or an expert to color and create something beautiful.
Seeing your finished coloring page provides
a sense of accomplishment.

Color Your Way to Better Branding

Create an Explainer Coloring Book that outlines your business process, shares industry-specific information and culture, or tells your business history —all with your branding.

PROMOTE YOUR BUSINESS

Our expert designers fully customize your Explainer Coloring Book by integrating your company colors, fonts, icons, and logos, so your brand is front and center.

EXPERT DESIGN

Our expert designers will work with you to create visually stunning coloring books that reflect your brand's culture.

CAPTIVATING STORIES

Our coloring books offer the option to include engaging and memorable stories about your business, providing a fun and interactive way for your customers to learn about your brand and develop a deeper connection with your company.

FUN & INTERACTIVE

Our books offer a fun and interactive way for your customers to engage with your business, whether coloring in your process, learning about your industry, or exploring your company's history.

culturetocolor.com | **cs@culturetocolor.com** | **386-309-2632**

QUESTIONS FOR LAVETA

☐ _____

☐ _____

☐ _____

☐ _____

☐ _____

☐ _____

☐ _____

✉ L@livinglegacieswithlaveta.com

www.ingramcontent.com/pod-product-compliance
Lightning Source LLC
Chambersburg PA
CBHW041134120626
46547CB00019B/2995